Health & Wellbeing 2

PSHE IN SCOTLAND

Curriculum for Excellence
CfE

Marel Harper, Gail Whitnall, Lesley de Meza
Stephen De Silva, Julie Ball & Fiona Young

DYNAMIC LEARNING

HODDER GIBSON
AN HACHETTE UK COMPANY

The Publishers would like to thank the following for permission to reproduce copyright material:
Photo credits Page 7 (top left) © Design Pics Inc. / Alamy; (centre) © Photofusion Picture Library / Alamy; (bottom right) © Mike Goldwater / Alamy; Page 9 © Photofusion Picture Library / Alamy; Page 12 (left) © Peter Barritt / Alamy; (right) © Ulrich Doering / Alamy; Page 13 (top) © Photofusion Picture Library / Alamy; (bottom) © Shenval / Alamy; Page 14 © Finnbarr Webster / Alamy; Page 18 (l to r) © TopFoto; © David Reed / Alamy; © Oleksiy Maksymenko / Alamy; © Les Cunliffe / Age Fotostock / Photolibrary.com; Page 19 (l to r) © VStock / Alamy; © Image Source / Alamy; © Sally and Richard Greenhill / Alamy; © Ingram Publishing Limited; Page 23 (left) © FRANCIS DEAN / Rex Features; (centre) © 2004 TopFoto / UPP; (right) © Chip Somodevilla / Getty Images; Page 24 from www.CartoonStock.com; Page 25 (top) © Imagestate Media; (right) © Imagestate Media; (bottom) © Imagestate Media; (left) © Tom Merton/Digital Vision/ Getty Images; Page 27 screenshot from www.watchyourspace.ie/Profile.aspx reproduced with kind permission of National Centre for Technology in Education, Dublin City University; Page 30 (top left) © Angela Hampton Picture Library / Alamy; (bottom left) © Alexander Caminada / Alamy; (right) © 2007 Todd Muskopf / Alamy; Page 33 (top) © Rex Features; (bottom) © Greg Baker/AP/Press Association Images; Page 34 (l to r) © aberpix / Alamy; © www.eyethinkphoto.com / Alamy; © South West Images Scotland / Alamy; © SHOUT / Alamy; Page 36 (top row, l to r) © Anna Stowe / Alamy; © Greg Balfour Evans / Alamy; © PCL / Alamy; (bottom row, l to r) © Ian Shaw / Alamy; © Alex Segre / Alamy; Page 37 (l to r) © Anna Stowe / Alamy; © Greg Balfour Evans / Alamy; © PCL / Alamy; © Ian Shaw / Alamy; © Alex Segre / Alamy; Page 43 (top row, l to r) © David Sacks / Getty Images; © Lisa Pines / Taxi / Getty Images; © Dave Nagel Photographer's Choice / Getty Images; © Debra McClinton / Stone / Getty Images; © Petrina Hicks / Stone+/ Getty Images; (bottom row, l to r) © STOCK4B / Getty Images; © Ryoko Uyama / Taxi / Getty Images; © Peter Dazeley / Photographer's Choice / Getty Images; © DK Stock/Veronique Krieger / Getty Images; Page 45 (top left) © mediacolor's / Alamy; (centre right) © Profimedia International s.r.o. / Alamy; (centre left) © ImageState / Alamy; (bottom right) © Image Source / Alamy; Page 46 (right) © Dennis MacDonald / Alamy; (left) © ClassicStock / Alamy; Page 47 (top) The Travel Library / Rex Features; (bottom) © Picture Partners / Alamy; Page 53 © Blend Images / Alamy; Page 56, screenshot from http://www.direct.gov.uk/en/YoungPeople/index.htm reproduced with kind permission by Directgov; Page 57 screenshot from Childline website http://www.childline.org.uk/Pages/Home.aspx reproduced with kind permission by the NSPCC; Page 58 Samaritans logo from http://www.samaritans.org/ reproduced courtesy of Samaritans; Page 59 Anti-Bullying Alliance logo from www.anti-bullyingalliance.org.uk reproduced courtesy of NCB; Childline logo from www.childline.org.uk reproduced with kind permission by the NSPCC; Action for Children logo from www.itsnotyourfault.org (National Children's Homes) © Action for Children; Think U Know logo from http://www.thinkuknow.co.uk/11_16/ reproduced courtesy of Thinkuknow - the education initiative delivered by the Child Exploitation and Online Protection Centre (www.thinkuknow.co.uk); Young Minds logo from http://www.youngminds.org.uk/ young-people/ reproduced with kind permission by YoungMinds; National Children's Bureau logo from www.youngncb.org.uk reproduced courtesy of NCB; Page 60 (top row, l to r) © Blend Images / Alamy; © Radius Images / Alamy; © Janine Wiedel Photolibrary / Alamy; (bottom row, l to r) © Luc Beziat / Stone / Getty Images; © Steve Stanford / Alamy; Page 62 (top left) © Angela Hampton Picture Library / Alamy; (bottom left) © Alexander Caminada / Alamy; (right) © 2007 Todd Muskopf / Alamy.

Acknowledgements p.23 Extract from *Two Weeks With the Queen* by Morris Gleitzman, published by Puffin Books (2003); **p.58** Samaritans case study based on information on www.samaritans.org and used with permission.

Every effort has been made to trace all copyright holders, but if any have been inadvertently overlooked the Publishers will be pleased to make the necessary arrangements at the first opportunity.

Although every effort has been made to ensure that website addresses are correct at time of going to press, Hodder Gibson cannot be held responsible for the content of any website mentioned in this book. It is sometimes possible to find a relocated web page by typing in the address of the home page for a website in the URL window of your browser.

Hachette UK's policy is to use papers that are natural, renewable and recyclable products and made from wood grown in sustainable forests. The logging and manufacturing processes are expected to conform to the environmental regulations of the country of origin.

Orders: please contact Bookpoint Ltd, 130 Milton Park, Abingdon, Oxon OX14 4SB. Telephone: (44) 01235 827720. Fax: (44) 01235 400454. Lines are open 9.00–5.00, Monday to Saturday, with a 24-hour message answering service. Visit our website at www.hoddereducation.co.uk. Hodder Gibson can be contacted direct on: Tel: 0141 848 1609; Fax: 0141 889 6315; email: hoddergibson@hodder.co.uk

© Lesley de Meza, Stephen De Silva, Julie Ball, Fiona Young, Gail Whitnall and Marel Harper (2009) 2010

First published as *PSHE Education 2* by Lesley de Meza, Stephen De Silva, Julie Ball and Fiona Young in 2009 by
Hodder Education,
An Hachette UK Company
338 Euston Road
London NW1 3BH

This edition first published 2010 by
Hodder Gibson, an imprint of Hodder Education,
An Hachette UK Company
2a Christie Street
Paisley PA1 1NB

Impression number   5 4 3 2
Year   2012

All rights reserved. Apart from any use permitted under UK copyright law, no part of this publication may be reproduced or transmitted in any form or by any means, electronic or mechanical, including photocopying and recording, or held within any information storage and retrieval system, without permission in writing from the publisher or under licence from the Copyright Licensing Agency Limited. Further details of such licences (for reprographic reproduction) may be obtained from the Copyright Licensing Agency Limited, Saffron House, 6–10 Kirby Street, London EC1N 8TS.

Cover photo © stockbroker/photolibrary.com
Illustrations by Richard Duszczak, and Oxford Designers and Illustrators
Typeset in 12pt Avenir by Fakenham Photosetting Limited, Fakenham, Norfolk
Printed and bound in Dubai

A catalogue record for this title is available from the British Library

ISBN: 978 1444 112 757

Contents

Chapter 1 Starting out
1. How will we work together? — 4
2. What's it like here? — 6

Chapter 2 Emotional health and wellbeing
3. What happens when we're feeling down? — 8
4. Is it good being me? — 10
5. Is anybody perfect? — 12

Chapter 3 Substance misuse
6. What about drugs? — 14
7. What about alcohol? — 16

Chapter 4 Relationships, sexual health and parenthood
8. Boys and girls – is there a difference? — 18
9. Sex – why all the fuss? — 20
10. What are HIV and AIDS? — 22
11. Nature or nurture? — 24

Chapter 5 Minimising harm
12. Social networks – what do I need to know? — 26
13. What can I do to keep safe? — 28
14. How can I keep safe on the inside? — 30

Chapter 6 Living in the world
15. How can we value each other? — 32
16. How can we challenge prejudice and discrimination? — 34

Chapter 7 Saving and spending money
17. What influences our spending? — 36
18. How can we save our money wisely? — 38
19. How can I budget successfully? — 40

Chapter 8 Mental and social wellbeing
20. What are emotions and how are they expressed? — 42
21. How should I respond to other people? — 44
22. How can I become the best I can be? — 46

Chapter 9 Planning for choices and changes
23. How do I work on my own and with others? — 48
24. What do I need to plan for? — 50
25. What are my career and future opportunities? — 52

Chapter 10 Support and information
26. When and where can we get help? — 54
27. Where can I find help on…? — 56
28. Young people's agencies – what do they do? — 58

Chapter 11 Review
29. What have I learned? — 60

Case studies for Lesson 14 — 62

1 Starting out

1 How will we work together?

In this lesson you will:
★ look back at the values of this PSHE course
★ create a group agreement so that the class can work together in a safe and positive way.

Rainbow values (from outer to inner):
- Know that each of us is unique
- Gain good information to make choices
- Develop decision-making skills
- Understand our emotions and feelings
- Enjoy what we learn
- Feel safe and supported to say what we think
- Listen to and consider what other people say

Source 1 PSHE values

Get Active 1

The rainbow in Source 1 shows the values that help us learn together in PSHE.

For each value, find someone in the class who has demonstrated it and give your reasons why you have chosen that person. You could present your findings in a table like the one below.

Find someone who …	Name	Reason
is unique.		
has gained good information in PSHE to help them make choices.		
has developed their decision-making skills.		
thinks they understand emotions and feelings better than they used to.		
enjoys learning.		
feels safe and supported to say what they think.		
listens to and considers what other people say.		

In Book 1, at the start of the PSHE course, you may have used the values on the rainbow diagram to create a group agreement so that everybody in the class could work together in a safe and positive way.

Here is an example of a group agreement that one class set up. It is based around the idea that everyone has both rights and responsibilities in PSHE.

> **GROUP AGREEMENT**
>
> I/We/Everyone in this group has the right:
> - to be listened to (only one person talks at a time)
> - to start on time
> - to privacy.
>
> I/We/Everyone in this group has the responsibility:
> - to listen to others
> - to arrive on time and be ready to start promptly
> - not to ask personal/private questions of others.

Get Active 2

1. Work together in pairs to come up with two more examples to add to the group agreement above. Remember to ensure that each right has a corresponding responsibility.
2. If you still have last year's group agreement, you should look at it, discuss it as a class and decide if you want to add to it. Alternatively, you may want to create a new agreement based on the example above.

As well as thinking about values, rights and responsibilities, you also need to understand the skills and attitudes your PSHE course will help you to develop and explore.

Get Active 3

Can you think of past activities in PSHE or other lessons that helped you learn more about:

- making choices
- making decisions
- dealing with emotions
- keeping healthy
- managing risks
- keeping safe?

Work in groups to write down one example for each.

Get Active 4

Of all the examples you discussed in Get Active 3, what has been the most useful to you personally and why?

2 What's it like here?

> **In this lesson you will:**
> ★ review the changes you have experienced in the last year
> ★ suggest ways of supporting pupils who are new to the school.

Starter activity

Think back to how you felt on your first day in First Year. You probably feel different now but in many ways you are still the same person. Complete these sentences, giving one reason for each:

1 We are the same as when we started in First Year because …
2 We are different from the way we were when we started in First Year because …

Many pupils arriving at secondary school do not know the buildings or people very well. Even if you had visited the school on some kind of induction programme, there was still a lot to take in.

Get Active 1

Think back over the things you experienced in your first few weeks as a new First Year pupil. Does anything in particular stand out in your memory? Can you remember how it felt?

In the Starter Activity and Get Active 1 you looked back at and started to think about what life was like in First Year. Throughout the rest of this lesson you will think about the current First Year newcomers to the school and how you could help them.

Many people going on a holiday or visiting a new place get a travel guide. The most useful guides are written by people who have actually experienced the place they are writing about. Imagine you had to write a 'rough guide' to the school for a new S1 pupil. What things does a new First Year pupil need to know? What would be useful? Look at the examples on page 7.

Names of the teachers

Guidance and/or year group systems

Moving around between lessons

Who to speak to if things go wrong

Where and when assemblies are held

Making new friends

The layout of the school and classrooms

How the canteen works

Lesson 2 What's it like here?

Get Active 2

Your task as a class is to write a guide to the school for a First Year pupil by following the steps below:

1 Make a list of things that you think are important to know about in the school. Use the examples above for ideas and come up with some of your own, which you may have discussed in Get Active 1. Each item on this list will form a chapter of the guide.
2 Work together in small groups to plan one section of the guide. Make a list of the information that you think needs to be included.
3 Feedback your ideas to the rest of the class.

Get Active 3

Consider all the different advice that your class came up with in the previous activity. Discuss whether there are any useful recommendations that your class could make to the School Council in order to help those who will join your school in future.

Get Active 4

In small groups, share with each other the thing that you found most useful in helping you to settle in at this school.

7

2.3 What happens when we're feeling down?

Emotional health and wellbeing

> **In this lesson you will:**
> ★ learn how our mental and emotional health affect our ability to lead fulfilling lives
> ★ learn that there is help and support available when our mental and emotional health is threatened
> ★ find out how and when to get help.

Starter activity

Sometimes things build up inside us so much that we think we might explode! Imagine blowing air into a balloon until that point where the air pressure inside is so great that the balloon can't take any more.

You can let the air out of a balloon to reduce the pressure. What can a person do to reduce the pressure on them and let their feelings out? Work in pairs to come up with some examples.

What does mental health mean? The charity Mind explains it like this:

The word 'mental' means 'of the mind'. It describes your thoughts, feelings and understanding of yourself and the world around you. The word 'health' generally describes the working order of your body and mind. So when we talk about 'mental health' we are referring to the working order of your mind.

Sometimes things go wrong with our bodies. We may catch a bug and become ill or we might get hurt in an accident. In the same way, we can have problems with our mental health.

Get Active 1

There's a big range of things that people might experience when their mental health is under pressure. For example, a person might feel very sad and want to cry, or perhaps think it's not worth getting out of bed in the morning. These feelings are perfectly natural and do not necessarily mean that someone is suffering mental ill health – but if those things continue for a while and build up then there might be a problem.

In groups, discuss and come up with other examples of the way mental ill health might show itself in people.

Joe's story

Joe had been off school for quite a while because he had to have an operation. While he was at home recovering, the family received some sad news – his grandma who lived abroad had died. Joe was sad that he would not see her again and knew that both his parents were really upset as well.

When he got back to school he was disappointed to find that his doctor wouldn't let him take part in any PE lessons – and even worse he couldn't play football so that meant he was no longer part of the school team.

To cap it all, Mark, his best friend, announced that he would be moving away at the end of term because his mother had a new job in another town.

Joe began to feel really depressed. He didn't look forward to going to school and he felt sad when he was at home. It seemed that everything he was used to was changing. His friends noticed he was becoming very quiet and keeping himself to himself.

Source 1

Get Active 2

Read Joe's story (Source 1) and work in pairs to discuss these questions:

1. Do you think Joe's feelings are a normal response to his situation?
2. Mark wants to support Joe but isn't sure how to start a conversation. How would you advise Mark to begin?
3. Who could Joe (or even Mark, on his behalf) turn to for help and advice?

It is natural to want help from other people when we experience difficult feelings and problems. But there are some things we can do to boost our own mental health (see Source 2).

Get Active 3

1. Look at the list in Source 2 and discuss why each item might help someone's emotional wellbeing.
2. Can you think of anything else that helps our emotional and mental health? Make a list of your ideas.

Get Active 4

How easy do you think it would be for someone in your school who was feeling down to be able to say so and ask for help? Give some reasons to explain your answer.

- ☐ Remember times when you felt safe and looked after.
- ☐ Make sure you get enough sleep.
- ☐ Try to eat healthily.
- ☐ Get enough exercise you enjoy, for example, swimming, skating, cycling.
- ☐ Spend time caring for something or someone else, for example looking after a pet, or helping a neighbour.
- ☐ Talk to someone who you feel close to.
- ☐ Spend time with good friends who are helpful and look out for you.

Source 2

From time to time we all need help from other people with our feelings and problems. If you are worried, cross or sad, talk to someone you trust. You can also call Breathing Space free on 0800 83 85 87, Childline free on 0800 1111, or Samaritans on 08457 90 90 90, or you can look up their local number in your phone directory.

Lesson 3 What happens when we're feeling down?

4 Is it good being me?

Chapter 2 Emotional health and wellbeing

> **In this lesson you will:**
> ★ recognise that the way in which you see your personal qualities, attitudes, skills and achievements affects your confidence and self-esteem
> ★ reflect on your own personal strengths and achievements.

Starter activity

Young people find it really easy to list all their faults and failings but they often find it difficult to see their good points. Working in pairs, take turns to tell your partner one thing about yourself that is good or positive.

Your partner may have used one of the words in Source 1 below. These are words that could be used when talking about yourself or others in a positive way.

Attractive
Beautiful
Cheerful
Delightful
Enthusiastic
Fair
Generous
Helpful
Important
Joyful
Keen
Lively
Marvellous
Natural
Overjoyed
Peaceful
Quick
Reflective
Self-confident
Tolerant
Untroubled
Valued
Wonderful
Xtra-special
Yummy
Zingy

Source 1

Get Active 1

1 Look at the list of words in Source 1. Choose three different words that match three letters in your name.
2 Work on your own to explain what each of the three words means and then try to think of a word that means the opposite of each.

There are two ways to balance the times when we are negative about ourselves. The first is to think about the positive ways to describe ourselves. The second is being honest about our positive qualities – don't be too shy to say when you are good at something. The game in Get Active 2 relies on you being honest and positive.

Get Active 2

Your teacher will give you some cards. Place the pile upside down in the centre of your group. The game is called 'Is it good being me?'. Listen carefully to the instructions on how to play. You are free to pass once if you can't think how to complete the sentence on the card, or you may ask other group members to help you.

If you have a positive attitude you are more likely to feel better about yourself and about life in general. Here are two statements that somebody could have made about the same situation:

Sometimes people use sayings to help them see the positive side of life. These include:

Get Active 3

The sayings above are great for helping an individual get a positive outlook on life. However, sometimes a whole group can become negative. As a class, discuss and come up with some mottos or sayings that could help your class stay positive and become the very best it can be.

Get Active 4

Is there a situation that you can remember when you did not feel positive about yourself? How could you look at it now in a more positive way?

Chapter 2 Emotional health and wellbeing

5 Is anybody perfect?

In this lesson you will:
★ look at how the way you see and feel about yourself is affected by a range of factors
★ look at differences between people and explore what 'empathy' means.

Starter activity

If you were asked to bring your favourite photograph of yourself into school, which one would it be? Describe it. For example:

- What are you doing?
- Is anyone else in it?
- Where was it taken?

The photographs and images we see in the media are usually of 'perfect' or 'beautiful' people. But there is also the saying that 'Beauty is in the eye of the beholder'. For example, look at the images on these two pages – each shows an image which different cultures and tastes would find beautiful.

Get Active 1

As a class, discuss the following questions:

1. Why do you think that the media usually shows 'perfect' or 'beautiful' people?
2. What do you think 'Beauty is in the eye of the beholder' means? Use the images on these two pages in your discussion.

12

Get Active 2

When talking about how people look and feel, the expression 'body image' is often used. What does it really mean?

Work in small groups to come up with some ideas of what 'body image' means to you.

People's body image is often influenced by the way others react to them. Different types of body sometimes attract attention and comment from others which isn't always positive. Comments can sometimes be cruel, but more often they are likely to just be thoughtless. When someone stops and imagines what it feels like to 'live in someone else's skin' they may be more considerate of the other person's feelings. We call this way of identifying with someone else's situation 'empathy'.

Get Active 3

Work in pairs to write an empathetic response to the problem page letters below.

Some good points in helping to express empathy:

- Try to avoid saying 'I know what it feels like … ' – everyone feels different.
- Be supportive in what you say rather than telling them what to do.
- If you can think of people or services that could offer help, you might want to mention them.

---

problem page

Dear Problem Page,

All my friends are allowed to wear make-up at weekends when we go out. They are experimenting with different types of lipstick and mascara. My family think make-up is not necessary for anyone and certainly won't let me use it. They are so old-fashioned! They might as well live on a different planet. I think I look awful without make-up and I want to keep in with my friends.

What should I do?

A.F.

Dear Problem Page,

During a sports event, I fell and broke one of my front teeth. The dentist has said I cannot have a crown on it until I am at least sixteen because my mouth is still growing and changing. I am so embarrassed and won't open my mouth to smile any more in case people laugh. I really hate how this makes me look.

What can I do?

B.T.

Get Active 4

From what you have learned in today's lesson, can you identify anything new about the way you might:

- look at yourself
- view others?

Lesson 5 Is anybody perfect?

3 Substance misuse

6 What about drugs?

> In this lesson you will:
> ★ think about the effect drugs can have on behaviour and the decisions people make
> ★ learn how drugs can lead to unplanned sexual activity
> ★ consider the long-term consequences of experimenting/using drugs.

Starter activity

In small groups brainstorm the different ways that drugs can affect behaviour and decisions.

Whose decision?

When you are at a party in a friend's house, are you always confident that no-one could have put a drug into your drink? Do you ever leave it unattended? Do you ever let anyone else get a drink for you? If you answered yes to any of these questions, then there is a chance that you could become a victim of drug-assisted sexual assault. Drug-assisted sexual assault, or drug rape as it is more commonly known, can be defined as the administering of a drug against an individual's wishes, or without their knowledge, which incapacitates or disorientates the individual with the intention of carrying out a sexual assault. This can happen to you whether you are male or female.

Get Active 1

1. Work together in groups to construct a checklist that all young people should follow to prevent their drink being 'spiked'.
2. Feedback and discuss your ideas with the rest of the class.

Get Active 2

1. In groups of 4 or 5 discuss what advice you would give to a person who thinks they have been drug-assisted sexually assaulted.
2. Feedback and discuss your ideas with the rest of the class.

Long-term consequences

The law divides drugs into three classes – A, B and C.

The Consequences			
Class	Drug	Possession	Production or dealing
A	Ecstasy, heroin and methadone, LSD, cocaine and crack, magic mushrooms, methamphetamine, PMA, 2CB, amphetamines (if prepared for injection).	Up to 7 years in prison, or a fine, or both	Up to life in prison, or a fine, or both
B	Amphetamines (speed), cannabis, synthetic cannabinoids (such as 'Spice'), pholcodine, methylphenidate (ritalin), mephedrone	Up to 5 years in prison, or a fine, or both	Up to 14 years in prison, or a fine, or both
C	Tranquilisers, some painkillers, GHB (gamma hydroxybutyrate), GBL (gamma Butyrolactone), BZP, Ketamine	Up to 2 years in prison, or a fine, or both	Up to 14 years in prison, or a fine, or both

> This is where you carry drugs that you're going to use yourself.

> If you're carrying drugs and it looks like you've bought them to sell, or give to your friends, you could be charged with 'possession with intent to supply' or 'supplying drugs'.

Source 1 (Adapted from KNOW THE SCORE, http://knowthescore.info/)

Remember: Having a criminal record can make it difficult for you to get a job or visa if you want to travel abroad.

Get Active 3

Look at Source 1 and think about the consequences for the people below:

1. Julie is stopped and searched by the police. She has ecstasy tablets for herself and friends in her pocket.
2. Robin has recently moved house after being charged with possession of Class C drugs. He has applied for lots of jobs but hasn't had an interview yet.
3. Mary and Douglas have four children and do not like their 16-year-old son's friends. He was charged recently with possession of drugs. Mary and Douglas have decided that they want the whole family to emigrate to Australia.

Get Active 4

Investigate local news reports from your own area. What reports have been made that make reference to substance misuse? What is your local community doing to address these issues?

Lesson 6 What about drugs?

7 What about alcohol?

> **In this lesson you will:**
> ★ find out some facts about alcohol use
> ★ consider how to make personal choices about safety, health and wellbeing
> ★ think about when and how to get help.

Starter activity

Think about some of the popular TV programmes that people watch regularly (for example soaps, dramas). Which ones have the characters meeting up in pubs, wine bars and clubs? How realistic is this?

Who is drinking alcohol?

A survey was taken of over 10,000 pupils aged 13 and 15 years old throughout Scotland in the autumn of 2008. The survey was confidential so nobody worried that the information could be traced back to them. Here are some of the findings:

- 89 per cent of 13 year olds said they had not drunk any alcohol in the past week. Contrary to media reports, we know that fewer young people aged 13–15 are drinking alcohol compared to 10 years ago.
- In the last 10 years, the proportion of pupils who have never drunk alcohol has risen. Most recent statistics say 48 per cent of 13 year old pupils said they had never had an alcoholic drink.
- 52 per cent of the youngest pupils who had drunk alcohol reported that they were allowed to drink at home at least sometimes.

Get Active 1

1. If someone based their views about young people and alcohol on what they heard and saw the media, what do you think they would say?
2. Read the information above about 'Who is drinking alcohol?'. Does it surprise you that so few young people of your age drink?
3. Imagine that you were invited to take part in a TV talk show about young people and alcohol. What would you say?

In Get Active 1 you found out that relatively few young people your age drink alcohol. However, as you get older many of you may find yourselves in situations where alcohol is available. On page 17 are some scenarios that young people say they have been in.

Get Active 2

Look at the scenarios below and, in groups, answer the questions.

The group always hung out together in the school holidays. This summer, one or two of them decided they wanted to see what getting drunk felt like. They didn't think they had drunk all that much but suddenly Joe passed out and collapsed on the floor. Nobody knew if it was the alcohol or if something else had gone wrong.

1. What advice would you give the group?
2. What should they do to help Joe?
3. What do you think they should say to Joe's parents?
4. What do you think they should say to their own parents?

Joe

Kira's parents are celebrating their wedding anniversary and are having a really big party. Kira and her brother have been allowed to invite some friends. Kira has asked Ashley, her best friend from school. Ashley is excited to be there but when Kira's mum offers her a glass of wine, Ashley doesn't know what to do. In Ashley's house, the children are never offered alcohol.

1. What does Ashley need to think about before making a decision?
2. What should she say to Kira's mum?
3. What do you think Ashley should say to her parents when she gets home?
4. Should adults offer alcohol to people under sixteen?

Ashley and Kira

Luci and Rob's dad drinks a lot of alcohol. He often gets very drunk and becomes angry and violent. Sometimes it is so bad he doesn't go to work. Their mum is worried sick about the family and is scared he is going to lose his job. Both the children are worried and want to do something to make things better.

1. What advice would you give Luci and Rob?
2. How could they help their mum?
3. How could they find out where to get help?
4. If the children hadn't talked to each other about their worries, who else could they have talked to?

Luci and Rob

Get Active 3

At the beginning of this lesson you talked about TV characters meeting up in pubs, clubs and wine bars. You could end up thinking alcohol is a regular part of everybody's life! We know this isn't really the case and the majority of people don't spend all their leisure time drinking. If you were asked to create a new TV soap, where would you set the main action? It needs to be in walking distance of their homes and a place where the characters can meet on a regular basis.

Get Active 4

If you wanted to find out more information on alcohol for yourself, a friend or a member of your family, where would you go or who could you talk to?

Lesson 7 What about alcohol?

4.8 Boys and girls – is there a difference?

Relationships, sexual health and parenthood

In this lesson you will:
★ think about the influences on boys and girls as they grow up
★ consider how you feel about being a girl/boy.

Source 1

Starter activity

From the moment you are born, manufacturers start labelling a lot of what you need into boys' and girls' categories. For example, as you can see in Source 1, pink is frequently used as the colour basis for 'girls' toys' and primary colours (red, blue and yellow) feature more for 'boys' toys'. In what other ways have you noticed that things for boys and girls appear to be different?

As well as things like toys and clothes being aimed at either boys or girls, the language we use with children from an early age can be different for boys and for girls. You may have heard some of these expressions and sayings:

- Big boys don't cry.
- Boys are made of slugs and snails and puppy dogs' tails.
- Be ladylike.
- Girls are made of sugar and spice and all things nice.

Expressions and sayings can influence the way we see ourselves growing up as boys and girls, men and women. These are called 'gender messages' – they are often about the different roles for males and females and can come from various places, for example:

- Home – parents, siblings and other relatives
- Social life – friends, other people of your own age
- Media – adverts, television, cinema, Internet, magazines
- Toys – computer games, sports equipment, children's play things
- School – teachers, textbooks, sports
- Culture – religion, ethnic group, traditions

Get Active 1

Work together in groups to come up with examples of different 'gender messages' from each of the places in the list above.

The messages that you have been looking at can sometimes end up becoming stereotypes. Boys and girls can believe they have to fit into a particular role – even when they don't feel that way themselves.

Source 2

Source 3

Source 4

Source 5

Get Active 2

1. Look at the photos (Sources 2–5). How does each illustrate the idea of male and female stereotypes?
2. Look at the statements below. For each one, decide whether you agree or disagree with it, or are not sure.
    - Girls are too emotional.
    - Boys who cry are wimps.
    - Girls are better at talking about their feelings than boys.
    - Boys are more logical than girls.
    - Girls need someone strong to protect them.
    - Boys can be just as caring as girls.

Get Active 3

Complete the following sentences:

- The best thing about being a boy/girl is …
- I don't like the way girls/boys are expected to …
- I think that boys/girls should be able to …

Lesson 8 Boys and girls – is there a difference?

19

9 Sex – why all the fuss?

> **In this lesson you will:**
> ★ learn how the body becomes sexually mature
> ★ think about what people should consider before starting to have a sexual relationship
> ★ consider how to help parents talk to their children about sexual relationships.

Starter activity

What do you think of when you hear the words 'human reproduction' and 'contraception'?

In the Starter Activity, you probably began to realise that human reproduction is about a lot more than just sexual intercourse. However, understanding how your body works and is changing is important too.

During puberty, our bodies change so that when we are adults we can have sexual intercourse if we want to. In puberty, our bodies produce hormones that make us feel different from before – and those differences will include having sexual feelings.

In Second Year you are too young to have sexual intercourse. The law says sixteen is the age at which a person can have sex – but that doesn't mean you *have* to!

Get Active 1

Below and opposite are lists of words for parts of female and male bodies. Copy the diagrams of the woman and man in Sources 1 and 2. Work in pairs and see how many of the parts of the diagrams you can label, using the words in the list.

Female

Clitoris – a small bump about the size of a pea above the urethra. It contains lots of nerve endings and gives sexual feelings.

Urethra – the opening that urine (wee) comes out of.

Vagina – the opening passage through which menstrual blood passes, in which sexual intercourse takes place and through which a baby is born.

Male

Foreskin – a layer of skin that covers the end of the penis. Some males have the foreskin removed for health or religious reasons – this is called circumcision.

Penis – the organ that hangs in front of the scrotum. There is a small opening at the tip of the penis, which is the urethra.

Scrotum – a sack of soft skin that covers and protects the two testicles, often called 'balls'.

Urethra – the narrow tube, inside the penis, that carries sperm and urine out of the body.

Sexual intercourse is often called 'making love'. It's a pleasurable feeling so most couples want to do it often. Couples who want to have intercourse don't always want to have a baby. To prevent getting pregnant, people use contraception. There are lots of different sorts of contraceptives and they work in all sorts of different ways. Some people don't like to use contraceptives for religious or other reasons.

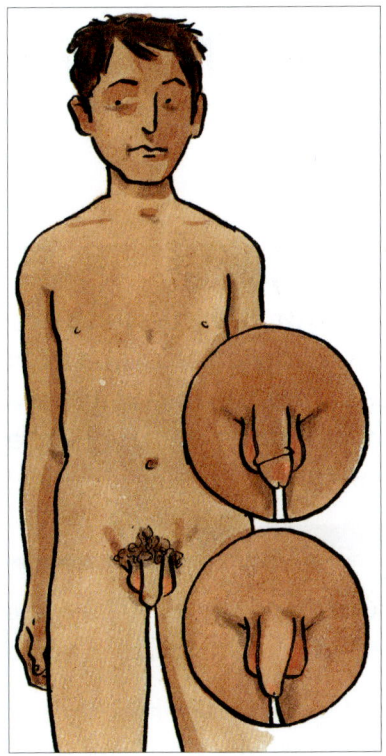

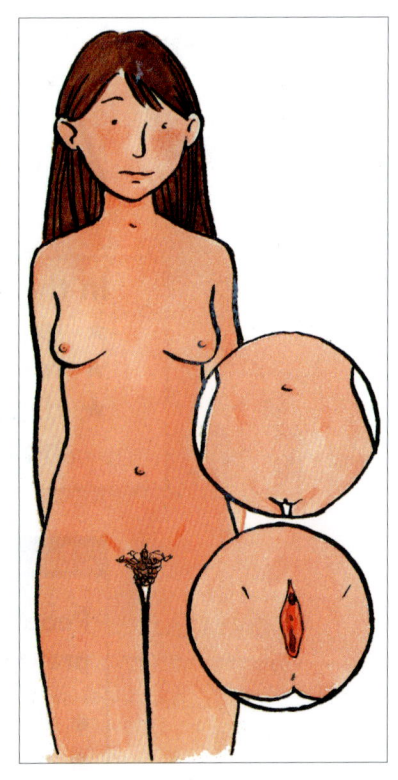

Source 1

Source 2

Get Active 2

There are lots of things to consider before starting to have sex. Work together in a group to give some examples of what two sixteen-year-old people should:

- think about
- know about
- be able to say

before they choose to start a sexual relationship.

Some people get embarrassed at even the thought of talking about sex – and yet sex is the most natural thing in the world. Most people's parents have had sexual intercourse – it is how we are made! If you want to know more about sex and relationships, then your parents are a good place to start. But what if you are someone who truly feels unable to discuss sex with your parents? Who else could you talk to?

Get Active 3

Work in pairs to identify a list of adults who you think would be easy to talk to about sex and relationships.

Get Active 4

If you were going to advise a parent about how to talk with their child about sex and relationships, where would you tell them to begin?

Lesson 9 Sex – why all the fuss?

10 What are HIV and AIDS?

In this lesson you will:
★ learn about the meanings of HIV and AIDS
★ research some facts about HIV and AIDS
★ discuss how people can be affected by prejudice and how this might be challenged.

Starter activity

People who have HIV or AIDS sometimes experience a lot of prejudice. Work with another person to:

- think of examples of how these prejudices might be shown
- give reasons why you think this happens.

Human	Only affects people
Immunodeficiency	Stops the immune system working properly
Virus	A living cell that can transmit infections
Acquired	Does not occur naturally – you get it from someone or somewhere else
Immune	The body system that fights illness and infections
Deficiency	Not fully functioning or working
Syndrome	A collection of illnesses or conditions

Source 1

Get Active 1

Read Source 1 on the left which describes and explains HIV and AIDS and then look at the statements (a–h) below. Sort the statements into three groups:

✓ True
✗ Untrue
? Uncertain

a) HIV only affects gay men and people who inject illegal drugs.
b) More than 73,000 people in the UK are living with HIV.
c) You can become infected with HIV if you share food and cutlery with someone who has the virus.
d) The red ribbon is an international symbol of support for people living with HIV and AIDS.
e) HIV is increasing in every region of the world.
f) You cannot get HIV from swimming pools.
g) HIV and AIDS cannot be cured.
h) In the UK, there are about 4500 children and young people under nineteen years old living with HIV.

Get Active 2

There may be some statements from the previous activity that no one is sure about. Use the following websites to do some research:

www.avert.org/young.htm
www.cwac.org/education_faq.htm
www.worldaidsday.org
www.tht.org.uk/informationresources/hivandaids/

Does your research leave you with any unanswered questions about HIV and AIDS?

In addition to facts and figures about HIV and AIDS, people have also written stories and poems about living with HIV. These tell the human side of the story.

Source 2 is an extract from *Two Weeks with the Queen* by Morris Gleitzman (something you might want to read on your own), which is about a boy called Colin.

In this extract, Colin hears some news about Griff.

'... Griff hasn't just got cancer. He's got cancer because he's also got a virus called AIDS.'

Colin had heard about that. The government had sent a booklet around about it. He knew it was a virus a lot of people were very scared of ...

'Want some?' Griff held out half a tangerine ... 'Or would you rather peel your own?'

Colin knew why Griff was giving him the choice. Some people were scared a person with AIDS could give it to you real easy, like a cold or nits. Ted had explained that you could only catch it off stuff from inside the body, blood and stuff like that.

'Thanks,' said Colin. He took the half tangerine.

They talked for ages.

Source 2

Get Active 3

Read Source 2 and work in pairs to discuss these questions:

1. Why are some people prejudiced towards those who, like Griff, have HIV or AIDS?
2. How do you think this prejudice makes a person who has HIV or AIDS feel?
3. How does it make others who hear these prejudiced comments feel?
4. What could your class, your school or your community do to try and stop prejudice towards people with HIV and AIDS?

Get Active 4

What could you do or say if you heard someone making an unkind and prejudiced remark about a person with HIV?

The red ribbon has been an international symbol of HIV for almost twenty years. World AIDS Day, 1 December each year, is a chance to show support for the 40 million people living with HIV worldwide.

Many famous people such as the actor Sir Ian McKellen are happy to promote HIV and AIDS awareness.

HIV and AIDS affects everyone across the world.

Lesson 10 What are HIV and AIDS?

11 Nature or nurture?

> In this lesson you will:
> ★ think about how we develop
> ★ learn about human behaviour and development
> ★ learn about the support and care required from a parent/carer to ensure that a child is nurtured.

Starter activity

1 What do you think is meant by the phrase 'nature or nurture'? Discuss and agree on a class definition. Your teacher will display the agreed meaning on the board flipchart paper.
2 As a class identify whether the following statements support the nature or nurture debate.
   a) I am tall – just like my biological father
   b) I don't like others to feel sad – my teacher has taught me how to show I care
   c) I don't ever cry – my dad thinks this makes me look soft
   d) I have blue eyes – just like my sister and mother
   e) There is a history of breast cancer in my family

Did the class agree? Were any statements considered as both nature and nurture?

From the moment we are conceived until we die we continuously develop. There are four main strands of development. These are physical, cognitive, emotional and social.

Get Active 1

1 Look at Source 1 and discuss the different ways that you have developed since you were born.
2 Record and display these for the class to see.

Get Active 2

Look at what the class recorded in Get Active 1. Decide whether these can be explained by nature or nurture. Can any be described by both terms?

Well, you walk like a duck, you quack like a duck... May I ask who brought you up?

PHYSICAL
The way that our bodies grow and change, e.g. growing taller, getting heavier. It is also about how we move around, pick things up, hold things etc.

COGNITIVE
The way we learn to think and reason, develop knowledge and understanding of things.

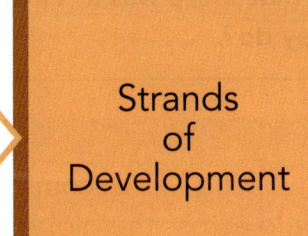

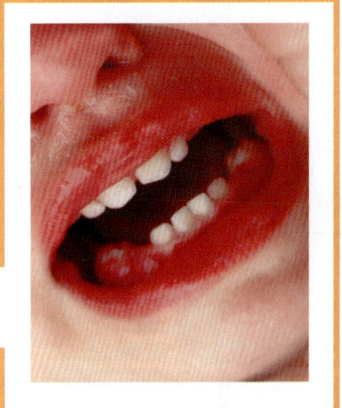

EMOTIONAL
Learning about feelings, like being happy or sad, falling in love, being angry and how we respond to those feelings.

SOCIAL
Learning to be with other people, to share, to play with and to get along with others.

Strands of Development

Source 1

Get Active 3
What support do you think is required from a parent/carer to ensure that a child is nurtured through the different strands of development? Create a checklist for new parents/carers to follow.

Lesson 11 Nature or nurture?

25

5 Minimising harm

12 Social networks – what do I need to know?

In this lesson you will:
★ learn about international Internet safety
★ identify how to keep safe and minimise harm online
★ research ways to reduce online risk and advise others about it.

Starter activity

If you heard that there was a 'Virtual Global Taskforce', what would you think they do?

Social networking has become a part of everyday life for many people across the globe. You can talk to anyone, anywhere, anytime online. This is an amazing use of technology. However, just like anything else, fantastic inventions can also end up being misused.

Research says that more than a quarter of eight- to eleven-year-olds claimed to have a profile page on a social networking website. This is despite age restrictions aimed at preventing pre-teens from using such sites.

MySpace says its users should be at least fourteen to register, while on Facebook and Bebo, users should be at least thirteen.

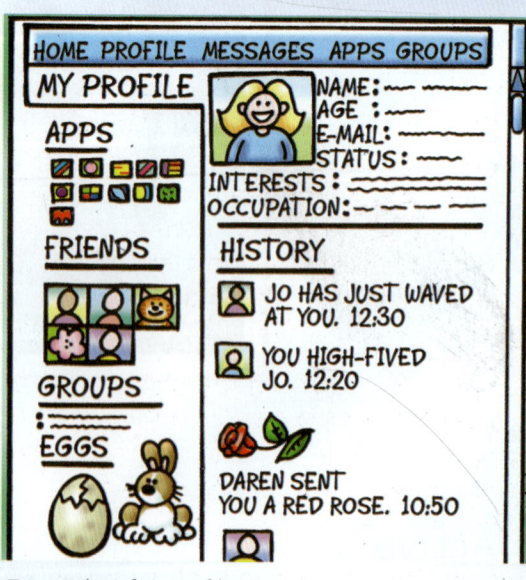

Example of a profile page

Get Active 1

You are at, or approaching, the age when you may choose to sign up to a social networking site. In preparation for that, here are some recommendations that are worth considering. Work together in small groups to explain why it is important to follow these guidelines.

a) Be as anonymous as possible.
b) Protect your information.
c) Be honest about your age.
d) Think before posting any photos.
e) Avoid in-person meetings.
f) Check comments regularly.

Get Active 2

Go to www.childnet-int.org/yourcall/ and try out the quiz that is all about using the Internet safely.

Experiment with different answers to see which would help you keep as safe as possible while still enjoying the Internet.

Get Active 3

1 Using the information from the previous activities, design a page for your school's website or handbook which explains how to use social networking sites safely.

2 More information about safe blogging can be found at www.watchyourspace.ie/Profile.aspx. This is an Irish website that was developed with Childline (see a screenshot from the website in Source 1).

   a) Why do you think that the image on the screenshot was chosen? What is it trying to show?
   b) Visit the website. How do the suggestions on the website help somebody take control of their profile?

Get Active 4

The Virtual Global Taskforce (VGT) is made up of law enforcement agencies from around the world. The aim of the VGT is to build an effective, international partnership of law enforcement agencies that helps to protect children online. The objectives of the VGT are:

- to make the Internet a safer place
- to identify, locate and help children at risk
- to hold perpetrators appropriately to account.

If you could invent a motto for the Virtual Global Taskforce, what would it be?

Source 1

Lesson 12 Social networks – what do I need to know?

13 What can I do to keep safe?

Chapter 5 Minimising harm

In this lesson you will:
★ consider some basic health and safety ideas for yourself and others
★ think about your own personal safety
★ learn about some basic first aid – the recovery position.

Starter activity

Here are three examples of when health and safety must be considered – for your protection and everyone else's:

1 A group of your friends have a day out cycling.
2 Your youth group spends the day travelling the canal on a barge.
3 You are volunteering to help clean up around the local woods and fields with a conservation group.

Come up with at least three safety rules to follow for one of these situations.

Safety rules apply to individuals as much as groups.

Look at the safety suggestions in Source 1 from teenagers who were concerned about their personal safety.

THINK TWICE ABOUT USING THE LATEST PHONE MODEL, MP3 PLAYER AND SO ON IN PUBLIC PLACES. EXPENSIVE EQUIPMENT COULD ATTRACT THIEVES AND MUGGERS!

ON BUSES, TUBES OR TRAINS, SIT NEAR THE DRIVER OR GUARD!

YELL IF YOU ARE THREATENED. AND IF POSSIBLE RUN AWAY!

NEVER HITCHHIKE OR ACCEPT RIDES FROM STRANGERS. TRY TO AVOID WALKING HOME ALONE!

IF YOU ARE BEING FOLLOWED, GO INTO A SHOP, OR TOWARDS PEOPLE. TRY CROSSING THE ROAD TO SEE IF THE PERSON FOLLOWS!

AVOID SHORT-CUTS THROUGH DARK OR DESERTED PLACES!

KEEP YOUR MOBILE HIDDEN WHEN YOU'RE NOT USING IT!

DO NOT WEAR AN MP3 PLAYER/PERSONAL STEREO BECAUSE IT STOPS YOU BEING AWARE OF WHAT IS HAPPENING AROUND YOU!

IF SOMEONE ASKS YOU FOR DIRECTIONS AND THEY MAKE YOU FEEL UNCOMFORTABLE, KEEP YOUR DISTANCE AND WALK AWAY!

AVOID EMPTY CARRIAGES ON TRAINS!

Source 1

Get Active 1

In small groups, discuss the safety suggestions in Source 1 and agree under which of the following three headings each one should appear:

- Travelling safely
- Feeling under threat
- Looking after personal possessions

Get Active 2

Use the ideas from the previous activity to help you think further about keeping safe. Decide a key safety message you would give to a primary school child who:

1 arrived home and found that no one was in.
2 got separated from an adult while out shopping.
3 was offered an ice-cream by a stranger while playing in the park.

As you get older you'll become more aware of how to help yourself and others. In last year's course you may have learned about making an emergency call by dialling 999. Here's some more potentially life-saving information:

- If someone collapses, get medical help (and if you know that they've taken pills or alcohol, tell the ambulance crew when they arrive).
- While someone else is calling for help, you could try to put the person into the recovery position (see Source 2).

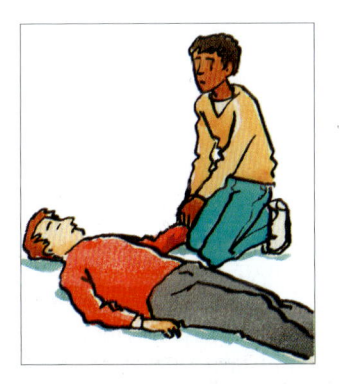

1. Place the arm nearest you at a right angle to the person's body.

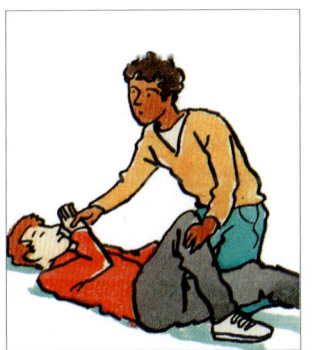

2. Bring the far arm across the person's chest and place the back of their hand against their cheek. Bend the person's far leg at the knee.

3. While keeping the person's hand pressed against their cheek, pull the knee towards you, rolling the person towards you and onto their side.

4. Stay with the person until help arrives.

Source 2

Get Active 3

In pairs, practise putting each other into the recovery position.

Get Active 4

Of all the new information you have learned in this lesson, which one thing could be the most important for you personally?

14 How can I keep safe on the inside?

In this lesson you will:
★ look at the importance of emotional safety as well as physical safety
★ think about ways people can make decisions about their safety
★ identify some ways of dealing with stress.

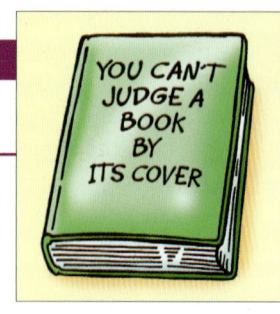

Starter activity

YOU CAN'T JUDGE A BOOK BY ITS COVER

What do you think this expression means?

Get Active 1

1 Read about the people in the profiles on this page. They are all about your age and you will probably notice they have some similarities to you. They are all basically happy people, but remember – don't judge a book by its cover.

After you have read the profiles, answer these questions, giving reasons for your answers:

Could these people:
- be pupils at your school?
- have similar hobbies and interests to yours?
- face similar challenges to you?

2 Now read the case studies on page 62 and answer the questions that follow them.

3 Revisit your answers to the questions in part 1 of this activity. Do you want to change your answers at all now that you have more information?

1 Zachary is thirteen years old and lives with his dad. He has lots of friends and his favourite sport is street hockey. He spends several evenings a week playing with his mates after school. He enjoys school and does well in nearly all his subjects.

2 Tyler and Laurie are fourteen-year-old twins who live with their mum and dad. The twins have always been popular and have good friends. The family have just moved to a new town and the twins are a bit nervous but looking forward to joining their new school and meeting new people.

3 Phoenix is twelve and is the youngest of three children, the baby of the family. They all live with their mother. Phoenix did well in First Year at school but now that his older brother and sister have left, he wonders what it will be like in Second Year.

You've just looked at three situations in which people about your age felt stressed and worried. They weren't necessarily everyday situations, but you can feel stressed over all sorts of things – sometimes even the smallest thing. You may feel that your friends have better clothes, shoes or computer games than you do. Someone at home may be really irritating you. You may feel that everyone in class understands things better than you and that you are not doing as well as them. It could be anything.

A good way of reducing stress is to look out for warning signs. Here are some of the things people say are warning signs for them:

Moodiness

Headaches

Short temper

Stomach pains

Over-reacting

Shutting yourself off from others

Feeling unhappy without knowing why

Get Active 2

1. What do you think stresses out people of your age?
2. Look at the warning signs of stress in the illustrations above. Can you think of any other warning signs that people might have?
3. Would you know what your own warning signs are?
4. Who could someone talk to when they notice their stress warning signs?
5. What could they do apart from talking to someone?

Get Active 3

Imagine what for you would be the most wonderful place on earth. What would make it a stress-free zone for you? Either draw it or describe what it looks like.

Get Active 4

Think back over this lesson – what would be your golden rule for keeping safe on the inside?

Lesson 14 How can I keep safe on the inside?

31

15 How can we value each other?

In this lesson you will:
★ examine the communities that you belong to
★ explore similarities and differences between yourself and others
★ consider how you can learn about and value the similarities between people.

Starter activity

Your teacher will ask you to go and stand in a range of varying groups.

Did anyone stay in the same group? It is important to remember that we are all different in many ways but that we also share things.

Family

Country

School

Culture/religion

Neighbourhood and district

Source 1

6 Living in the world

Lee Mei is a thirteen-year-old girl – that's her in Source 1. As you can see, she belongs to a variety of communities:

- She is a member of the Lee family. (In Chinese culture the family name comes before the given [first] name.)
- She is a member of S2 at Springfield High School.
- She lives in a semi-detached house in the West End of Glasgow.
- She and her mum, dad and brother are Buddhists.
- She is a British citizen and has a United Kingdom passport.

Get Active 1

Everyone belongs to more than one community. Draw a diagram either like Lee Mei's opposite, or of your own design to represent you and the different communities you belong to.

Even though people live their lives in different types of communities, we all share similar experiences. For example, everyone has a birthday, people have favourite or special foods, most people enjoy some kind of community celebration once a year, people mark special stages in their lives with parties and ceremonies, etc. In Get Active 2 is an example of individual people who, although they may appear 'different', actually share important similarities with each other.

Get Active 2

Rebecca Adlington and Sam Hynd are both swimmers. Rebecca won a gold medal at the Beijing Olympics in 2008, and Sam won a gold medal at the Beijing Paralympics in 2008. Can you think of other ways in which people who appear different at first glance, may share similarities?

Rebecca Adlington

Get Active 3

Work together in a small group and discuss the following topics – see if you share any similarities across the whole group.

- One festival/celebration that you all take part in.
- One healthy food that you all enjoy eating.
- One achievement you've all experienced since joining this school.
- One badge/charity bracelet that you would all be proud to wear.

Sam Hynd

Get Active 4

Complete this sentence: 'I share … with the entire human race and I am also unique and special because … '

Lesson 15 How can we value each other?

Chapter 6 Living in the world

16 How can we challenge prejudice and discrimination?

In this lesson you will:
- ★ find out what 'prejudice' and 'discrimination' mean
- ★ think about different types of prejudice
- ★ consider how to challenge prejudice and discrimination assertively.

Starter activity

Look at the photographs below – they are what you would probably see and experience in any local town or city. They don't present a challenge to the majority of people, but they could cause problems for others. Who do you think might have difficulties and why?

People who have particular needs or disabilities can find that their needs when moving around town are not taken into consideration. Worse still, other people may decide they know what's best for someone else. 'Prejudice' literally means to pre-judge people based on what a person *thinks* they know about them. For example, some older people might think that teenagers hanging around in their local shopping centre must be up to no good, even if they aren't.

All sorts of people may experience prejudice because others don't bother to get to know them, or find out about them.

34

Get Active 1

What sorts of prejudice might the following people experience from others in our society?

a) A person with visual impairment (blind person).
b) A person who uses a wheelchair to get around.
c) A person who cannot read or speak English.
d) A teenage 'hoodie'.
e) A person who looks different from the majority of people around them because of the clothes they are wearing or the way they wear their hair.

Prejudice can lead to people being discriminated against. Discrimination means treating somebody differently because of something about them. Below are some words that describe different types of prejudice.

| Ageism | Sexism | Racism | Homophobia |

Get Active 2

What types of prejudice do the words above refer to? In pairs, come up with a definition for one of the terms and give examples of how this prejudiced attitude could lead to somebody being discriminated against.

Get Active 3

Imagine your local newspaper has recently published a series of articles about prejudice and discrimination in the community. Choose one of the newspaper headlines below and write a letter to the editor explaining why you think this prejudice needs to be challenged.

Fit and healthy but too old to be on lollipop patrol

Woman 'brickie' told to put up with the lads' wolf whistles

Insulting graffiti sprayed in Muslim cemetery

Nurse refuses to work with gay doctor

Get Active 4

If you could do one simple thing to challenge prejudice, what would it be and how would you do it?

17 What influences our spending?

In this lesson you will learn:
★ some of the reasons why we spend money
★ how we choose to support different kinds of shops
★ how price and competition affect our consumer decisions
★ how our consumer decisions affect other people.

Starter activity

Why do we spend money? In pairs, list all the things you've bought over the last week. Then discuss how much you needed the things, and whether they were luxury or impulse purchases.

The Starter Activity should have got you thinking about what people of your age spend their money on and why. You are consumers and have choices about what you buy and where you buy things. You make decisions that have an impact on the economy.

Get Active 1

1. As a class, brainstorm all the different types of shops you can think of.
2. Now look at how you decide where to shop. Imagine you are a typical customer at each of the shops shown below. In pairs, list all the reasons why you'd choose to shop at each, then give feedback to the class.

Small independent local grocery shop

Large out-of-town supermarket

Designer boutique

Local speciality shop

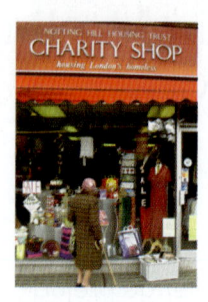

Charity shop

Your decision on where to spend your money doesn't just affect that particular shop. It also affects all the suppliers who provide goods and services to those shops; and it affects the other shops that you choose *not* to use. The different effects are shown in the table opposite.

Saving and spending money

Shops	Small independent grocery shop	Large out-of-town supermarket	Designer boutique	Local speciality shop	Charity shop
Suppliers	Medium and mass market suppliers	Mass market suppliers from across UK and abroad	Design industry (clothing and goods)	Individual or small-scale suppliers from locality	People donating goods
		Advertising industry	Advertising industry	Local advertising	
		Packaging industry	Packaging industry		
		Finance industry	Finance industry		

Get Active 2

Look at the table above and answer the following questions:

1. What would happen if consumers could get all they needed at the supermarket, and stopped using the small independent grocery shop and local speciality shops?
2. If everyone started to buy at the charity shop and no one went to the designer boutique, what might be the effects?

Get Active 3

1. In Get Active 1, you looked at what factors affect our decisions as to where to shop. As a class, discuss whether price is the most important of all those factors.
2. If price is important, imagine what would happen if one supermarket chain slashed its prices for milk. In pairs, work out a possible chain reaction to these questions:
   a) Would people buy more milk there?
   b) What would happen to milk sales at other supermarkets and at the small grocery shop?
   c) Would these other shops put their prices down too? If not, how could they compete?
   d) What impact would this have on the dairy farmers who supply the supermarket?
   e) Would the consumer pay more for local milk?
   f) What might make milk prices go back up again?
3. When shops compete with each other over price, there are winners and losers. As a class, name all the possible winners and losers, giving an explanation for each one.

Get Active 4

On your own, list three things that you have learnt that a shop can do to persuade you to buy its goods rather than those from another shop.

Lesson 17 What influences our spending?

37

18 How can we save our money wisely?

In this lesson you will learn:
★ why we save money
★ which organisations help you to save money
★ how interest builds up over time.

Starter activity

1. Why do we save? In pairs, make a list of all the reasons why you might put money aside to save.
2. How many pupils in the class save some money each month?
3. Where do they save it?

We all need to save money in order to buy the things we want, to provide for a 'rainy day' and for when we stop working. Saving money requires discipline, but it has rewards and is a very useful life habit. Saving money in a piggy bank is a short-term measure, but it is wiser to get your money to 'work harder' by getting a savings account.

The main organisations that offer savings accounts are banks and building societies, some of which offer online savings accounts.

Get Active 1

1. Where would you go, if you had a substantial sum of money to save? List some names of each of the following kinds of organisation:
   - Banks
   - Building societies
   - Online savings companies

2. As a whole class, decide on the advantages and disadvantages of each kind of organisation. Some are given below as a starting point – decide which type of organisation they refer to.

Advantages ✓
- Conveniently located on high streets
- Owned by members not by shareholders
- Often offer higher rates of interest
- Offer a variety of products
- Can access your account anytime

Disadvantages ✗
- Difficult to deposit cash
- Sometimes do not offer good rates of interest
- Difficult to speak to anyone about your account

When you leave money in a savings account to grow over time you will be paid some extra money called 'interest'.

This interest is usually calculated as a percentage of the amount you put in. To help people decide where to save their money there are online comparison sites, which compare best rates offered by different financial organisations.

Get Active 2

1. Copy and complete the table, working out how much money you would have at the end of a year in each of the savings accounts.
2. What factors do you think influence the rate of interest?

Type of account	Rate of interest	Amount earned in Year 1	Conditions of account
Current account £1000	1%		no conditions
e-saver account £1000	5%		all dealings online
Monthly saver account £1000	7%		monthly deposits, no withdrawals
Savings bond £1000	8%		two-year fixed rate account, with no withdrawals

Get Active 3

1. Imagine you had £1000 and were prepared to save for three years. Complete the table below to find out what interest you make.

	Starting amount	Interest at 10%	Total by end of year
Year 1	£1000	£100	£1100
Year 2	£1100		
Year 3			

2. By what percentage has your original saving grown after three years?
3. Why is it more than ten per cent growth?

Get Active 4

Earning interest on savings is only one of the ways to save more money.

1. Make a list of ways in which you could:
   - spend less
   - earn more
   - invest money in other ways.
2. What are the advantages and disadvantages of each?

Lesson 18 How can we save our money wisely?

19 How can I budget successfully?

> **In this lesson you will learn:**
> ★ that managing your money can help you buy more of the things you want
> ★ how budgeting can help you set and achieve financial goals
> ★ how to set up a budget and cope with the unexpected.

> **Starter activity**
>
> 1 Can you ever have enough money? Before you answer this, discuss as a class the difference between spending on what you *need* and spending on what you *want*.
> 2 If you haven't enough money for everything, which should you make your higher priority: what you *want* or what you *need*?

Look at the questions below. Can you answer them easily?

- Do you know how much money you have coming in, and how much you regularly spend?
- How do you decide when to spend and when to save?
- Have you enough money left for treats after you have bought your necessities?
- How can you save for something in the future, if you can't afford it right now?

There's one tool that will help you answer all these questions, and it's called a *budget*.

The key idea of a budget is balancing what money goes out (your *spending*) against what money comes in (your *income*).

You could be in one of three positions:

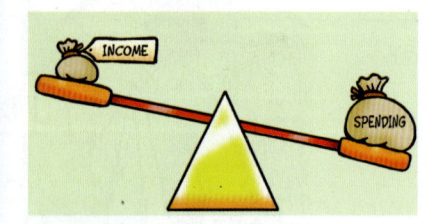

1 Your spending is more than your income.

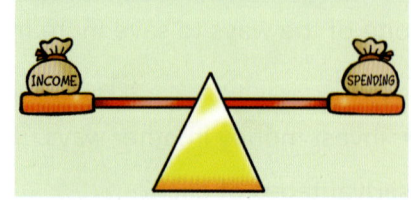

2 Your spending is exactly equal to your income.

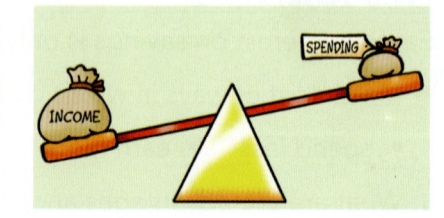

3 Your income is greater than your spending.

Get Active 1

Look at the seesaws opposite. As a class, discuss which are the worst and best positions to be in, and why.

If you manage to be in the third position, it means that you can save money for one-off purchases or events. In the next activity, you will help Sam to get into the third position so he can save money to go camping.

Get Active 2

In pairs, help Sam work out how he can afford to go away on a camping trip.

1. At present he spends all his income, so which position of the seesaw is he in?
2. He needs to save £20 in ten weeks, so how much does he need to save per week?
3. What are the different ways of saving this amount per week?
4. Copy and complete Table 1, filling in the figures for him.
5. Discuss your solutions with the class.

Current weekly income	£	Current weekly spending	£
pocket money	2	comic	1
money for odd jobs	2	pet food	1
		music	2
Total	4	Total	4
New weekly income		New weekly spending	
		weekly savings target	
Total		Total	

Table 1

Table 2 shows Sam's and his friends' budget for sharing equally the trip costs.

Original budget				
Income	£	Spending	£
Sam	20	petrol money for lift to and from the campsite	16
Friend 1	20	campsite fee	10
Friend 2	20	food etc at £10 each	40
Friend 3	20	entry money to local attraction at £2.50 each	
		ice creams at £1 each	
Total	80	Total	

Table 2

Get Active 3

1. In your pairs, use Table 2 to answer:
   a) How much will attraction entry total?
   b) Will ice cream blow the budget?
2. Suddenly one friend drops out. Table 3 shows how their income falls. The petrol money and the campsite fee are 'fixed costs' that can't be reduced, even if there are fewer people.
   a) Work out the rest of the budget.
   b) What effect does one person dropping out have on their budget?
   c) How could you balance the budget?

Revised budget			
Income	£	Spending	£
Sam	20	petrol money	16
Friend 1	20	campsite fee	10
Friend 2	20	food etc at £10 each	
		entry money to local attraction at £2.50 each	
		ice-creams at £1 each	
Total	60	Total	

Table 3

Get Active 4

1. Budgeting isn't boring – it's an aid to adventure. Explain why this is so.
2. How would you make sure your budget was robust enough to withstand a 'rainy day'?

Lesson 19 How can I budget successfully?

41

Mental and social wellbeing

What are emotions and how are they expressed?

In this lesson you will:
★ learn that your feelings and emotions are influenced by a variety of things
★ learn about expressing emotions in a variety of ways
★ identify positive ways to manage emotions and negative behaviours.

Starter activity

Take a couple of minutes to think of a time when you were very happy – an actual event. What happened? Who was there? Where did it take place? Now express the event as a human sculpture and explain the story behind your 'sculpture' to the other people in your group.

Get Active 1

Think about how you are feeling today. Think about it for a moment. Has anything happened that's affected how you feel? Express the emotions you have experienced today as a rainbow – writing what you felt in the most appropriate colour. Some examples are given below.

- The bus was late and I felt angry.
- Looking forward to breaktime made me feel a bit better.
- The weather is great and the sun is shining and I feel happy.
- I'm worried in case my maths homework isn't totally correct.
- Now it's raining I feel fed up.
- I always find English lessons make me thoughtful.
- Hooray, the end of the day – time to catch up with my mates.

In Get Active 1 you may have realised that throughout the day you go through lots of different emotions and that our feelings are affected by what we see, hear, touch, think about and even what we taste or smell.

When thinking about how we feel, it's helpful to be able to identify our feelings by name, and there are lots of words to express different emotions and degrees of an emotion (for example, cross, angry, livid, annoyed).

Source 1

Source 2

Source 3

Source 4

Source 5

Source 6

Source 7

Source 8

Source 9

Get Active 2

1 Look at the images in Sources 1–9. They show young people expressing different emotions through their body language and facial expressions. Can you identify the feelings they are showing by name? In groups of four, match the emotion listed below to the correct image. Explain your choices.

a) angry   c) chilled   e) surprised   g) happy   i) frustrated
b) sad   d) puzzled   f) mischevious   h) scared

2 We all know words like 'happy', 'angry', 'sad' and 'scared'. What other words can you think of to describe these four feelings?

Get Active 3

It is normal to experience all sorts of emotions – things like joy, excitement and delight as well as anger, hurt and frustration. Have you ever wanted to share your feelings with someone but were afraid to? What makes it difficult to share feelings?

Get Active 4

Of all the emotions that are difficult to share with other people, anger and frustration are often top of the list and they seem to cause the biggest problems. Working in pairs:

- Think about the things in your own lives that create anger and stress for you. In what ways have you reacted when you've felt angry or stressed?
- What more positive ways can you think of to 'let off steam'?

Get Active 5

What is one positive piece of advice you could give someone who is afraid of showing their emotions?

Lesson 20 What are emotions and how are they expressed?

21 How should I respond to other people?

> **In this lesson you will:**
> ★ learn about and practise some relationship skills
> ★ practise the skills of communication and negotiation
> ★ identify assertiveness skills.

Everyone has emotions and all sorts of things can trigger them. It is normal to experience a broad range of emotions during adolescence.

Whatever the emotions are – and however off-the-wall they might seem – they are very real when we experience them and therefore it is important to be aware of and to communicate our feelings. We also need to be responsible and to learn to control our reactions when our emotions feel like they're taking over!

Starter activity

Our non-verbal communication is, for many of us, as important as the words we use. Think of two emotions you have felt today. In pairs, take turns to mime these two emotions to one another. Can your partner guess what the two emotions you experienced were? If not, try again.

One way of being direct and honest in any relationship is to use an 'I feel' statement. This is particularly effective when you're dealing with problems in a relationship.

The situation in the cartoon could possibly have been turned around if instead of shouting at the borrower, the lender had explained how they felt. For example, 'When you didn't return my game for over two weeks I felt really angry and upset because it's valuable and important to me and I haven't finished the game yet.'

This would have given the borrower a chance to admit they hadn't thought about how the lender felt and, at the same time, apologise.

Get Active 1

In groups, look at the situations below and for each:

- come up with typical negative responses
- find ways to reach a positive solution with an 'I feel' statement.

a) A friend ignores you.
b) Your brother or sister borrows an item of clothing and doesn't return it.
c) You do all of your chores at home but your parent/carer doesn't thank you – they just give you even more to do.
d) A friend lies to you.
e) A member of your family takes something of yours without asking.

Example

Situation	Typical negative response	'I feel' statement
A friend continually interrupts you.	'Stop butting in. You are not the only one who wants to talk.'	'When you interrupt I feel hurt because I have something important to say, too.'

In the previous activity you found ways to tell people how you feel without hurting their feelings. Sometimes we behave in certain ways because we don't want to risk spoiling a relationship. It is, however, important to stand up for yourself and maintain relationships at the same time. The best way to do this is to be assertive. Some people get confused between aggressive and assertive behaviours. The differences are shown in the photos opposite.

Get Active 2

Imagine a situation in which one person has spread some gossip about another.

- What words and actions would an aggressive person use to express how they feel?
- What words and actions would an assertive person use to express how they feel?

Get Active 3

Look at the case studies your teacher will give you and in pairs, turn them into a storyboard or comic strip. It must describe in words and pictures a positive and assertive way to reach a solution that has a win-win outcome for everyone. Remember how useful it is to include 'I feel' statements.

Get Active 4

What personal behaviours could you work on so that you can stand up for what you believe in and care about?

Aggressive behaviour, as shown above, often includes shouting, pointing and invading someone's personal space. Aggressive language uses put-downs and insults.

Assertive behaviour, as shown above, often includes listening, speaking clearly and firmly without anger, respecting the other person and looking someone in the eye in a non-threatening way. Assertive language is honest without being hurtful.

Lesson 21 How should I respond to other people?

22 How can I become the best I can be?

In this lesson you will:
- ★ begin to develop the confidence to try out some challenges
- ★ think about your personal strengths and achievements
- ★ have an opportunity to present yourself positively
- ★ practise working together as a team.

Starter activity

You have just been told that a reporter from the local newspaper is visiting your school and you have been chosen to be interviewed as a positive model of young people today. The interview will start in under half an hour!

How would you feel if you heard this news? Do you think you would have any physical reactions that would give away your feelings?

Community challenge

Get Active 1

Now imagine that you and a team of three friends are preparing to audition for a reality television series called 'Community Challenge'. The show is about how teams from schools support people and groups who need help in their local community. The members of the winning group will be given a trust fund of money to pay for their university education or to set them up in business. The four of you really want to be contestants. What will you need to do to prepare for the audition?

You will need to consider the following:

- What will you say/do/wear?
- How will you convince producers of your sincerity?
- What talents and skills and personal qualities do you have as a group?
- What are your achievements as a group?
- How will you work as a team?

You finished Get Active 1 thinking about teamwork. The next activity encourages you to work as a team to present a good account of yourselves as representatives of your school.

Get Active 2

As members of the Scottish Youth Parliament, you have been invited to attend a meeting with the First Minister. It is a meeting at which pupils from schools all over the country will be given the opportunity to talk about what they gain from attending their school. What preparation do you think your group would need to make to give a clear account of your school and be good ambassadors for your school? Follow the steps below:

1. With your teacher, brainstorm interesting facts about your school. For example:
   - how it's run: School Council/House or Year groups/Tutor systems
   - specialist areas of learning
   - history of the school (for example, the age of the buildings)
   - what your school and its community do well
   - celebrated ex-pupils (we call these 'alumni').

2. Now go back to working in your groups from Get Active 1. Think about how you are going to prepare for the meeting with the First Minister. For example:
   - Who will talk about what? How will this be decided? Will people need to practise answering questions?
   - What will the representatives wear? If they are going to wear school uniform, who will be responsible for checking it?

3. Finally, find a way to describe to the First Minister how your school enables you to develop as one of the following:
   - Confident Individuals
   - Successful Learners
   - Effective Contributors
   - Responsible Citizens

Holyrood, the Scottish Parliament, in Edinburgh

So far in this lesson you have presented the best of yourselves as a team and represented your school in a positive way. The next activity is about you as an individual presenting the best of yourself to other people.

Get Active 3

Next year your school is organising a month-long exchange visit with pupils from a country that you have always wanted to visit. Your family is happy for you to go but cannot afford the total cost so you have asked a local company to sponsor you. The staff at the company want to meet you. You need to make a good impression and have been asked to create a personal profile to take with you. What will you say about yourself?

Look at the headings on the example personal profile on the right and use them as a starting point for your own profile.

Get Active 4

A spotlight has just been switched on and it's shining on you! You have been asked to complete the sentence: 'It's great to be me because ... '

Al Williams
22 Any Street, New Town, Anywherebury

Talents and skills
I can ride a horse and am quick and accurate with computer work

Personal qualities
Punctual and hardworking

Achievements
I won first place in the 50m front crawl at the school swimming gala

Best subjects
English, maths, PE and drama

Group memberships
New Town swimming club

Hobbies and interests
Horseriding and swimming

Lesson 22 How can I become the best I can be?

47

9 Planning for choices and changes

23 How do I work on my own and with others?

In this lesson you will:
★ identify some of the personal attitudes required in work
★ identify skills and attitudes in yourself and others
★ identify what enables you to learn successfully
★ understand the need to continue to develop your skills and learning throughout your life.

Starter activity
1 List jobs, paid and unpaid, that pupils in your class currently do.
2 What skills and attitudes are required for each job?

Skills are something you have learned to do the job well (such as managing money), whereas attitudes are the personal characteristics and behaviours you display (such as reliability). Both are important in the workplace.

Get Active 1
1 In pairs, imagine you're the boss. List attitudes you'd like in your staff.
2 If your staff have the right skills but the wrong attitudes, how successful will they be? Vote on which is more important: skill or attitude?

Learning about what motivates you and the things you are good at starts at school. Understanding the skills and qualities you already have and those you need to develop will help you make the right choices in the future.

Get Active 2
Individually, think about a recent piece of schoolwork you enjoyed doing. Answer the following questions.

1 What interested you in this work?
2 How did you organise yourself to do the work?
3 How did you feel as you carried it out?
4 Did you finish the work, and were you satisfied with it?
5 What skills and attitudes did you demonstrate? Sum this up in a list under the heading 'My qualities, attitudes and skills'.
6 Which of these skills would you like to develop? Write these in a second list entitled 'Qualities, attitudes and skills I would like to develop'.
7 How do you think these skills would be relevant to the world of work?

You'll succeed at what you enjoy

Learning doesn't stop when you finish school. You often have to go back to studying or training to further your career or change direction. Learning later on can be quite different from learning at school.

Get Active 3

1 How do you think you would find learning if you had to fit it in after work where there was no space or quiet?
2 How do you think you would find learning on your own, without the opportunity to discuss things face to face?
3 In pairs, list the attitudes and environment you think you need to learn successfully on your own.

Now look back at the two lists you started in Get Active 2 (parts 5 and 6).

5 Which of the attitudes that you have already shown you possess would help you to learn later on in life?
6 Which attitudes might you need to develop?

No space or quiet for studying

There is no job where you work entirely on your own. You will always be working with other people, even if it's via a phone or a computer, so you have to take other people's skills and attitudes into account.

Get Active 4

1 Look at the cartoon of the eight people at a meeting. Match the feelings below to the faces:

a) Bossiness   c) Shyness   e) Confusion   g) Nervousness
b) Boredom   d) Frustration   f) Eagerness   h) Involvement

2 In groups, discuss what it's like to work with other people. Focus on the issues below and then share your findings with the class.

- Compare how you feel and behave when you work in a) large groups b) in pairs and c) on your own.
- What skills and attitudes are useful for group, pair and solo work? Are different skills required?
- Which skills and attitudes do members need to develop in order for successful group work to take place?

Get Active 5

Look at your list of existing qualities, skills or attitudes. Select three that you think would be most useful to you when you work.

Of your list of qualities, skills and attitudes that you would like to develop, which three would be the most useful for work?

Successful group work depends on recognising different attitudes

Lesson 23 How do I work on my own and with others?

49

24 What do I need to plan for?

> **In this lesson you will learn:**
> ★ how we think about our abilities and how others regard our abilities
> ★ about self-confidence and getting to know ourselves
> ★ how to get the tools for a successful future
> ★ the importance of thinking about the future today.

Starter activity

How do you see yourself?

- 'Do it now' person
- 'Wait and see' person
- 'Think, plan and take action' person
- 'Take opportunities as they present themselves' person
- 'Head in the clouds' person

Compare with a partner. Do they see you differently?

At some point someone has probably told you off for 'only thinking about yourself' or being 'selfish'. They might have had a point!

However, 'believing in yourself' isn't always a selfish or 'bad' thing. Belief in yourself, or self-confidence, is a vital tool in life.

Get Active 1

1 Think about five positive things that describe the sort of person you think you are. Now think about the points you might like to change about yourself. Copy and complete the table below.

Positive points about the way I am now	Things about myself I want to change

2 How confident do you feel about changing? As a class, discuss what holds people back from being what they want to be.

Imagine the biggest and best luxury liner sailing across a calm sea. What do you think will happen if the mechanism for steering – the rudder – breaks? Your mind and willpower are your rudder. They steer you towards your destination.

Think about what sort of life you might like. For instance, do you want a career that allows you to:

- travel
- earn lots of money
- spend time with your family
- meet lots of interesting people
- help people
- follow a special interest?

Now consider what would happen if you didn't give your life or career any thought at all. Without plans, most people will drift eventually. If you want to succeed at something you enjoy, you need to think and make decisions about what you want to do.

Whatever you decide to do in life, in order to get there, you need basic skills in various areas, such as those shown in the pictures below. Plan to succeed by working towards developing these basic skills.

Punctuality

Appearance

Attitude

Written communication

Spoken communication

Get Active 2

1 Jim is going for an interview as an estate agent. Look at the first column of the table below. How could Jim show these skills to make a good impression on the person interviewing him? What would make the interviewer think twice before employing Jim? Copy and complete the table:

Areas in which skills are required	What creates a good impression?	What creates a bad impression?
Punctuality		
Appearance		
Attitude		
Spoken communication		
Written communication		

2 Discuss whether 'You only have one chance to make a first impression' is true.

Get Active 3

The Latin expression, 'Carpe diem' means 'Seize the day' or 'Do it now'. Discuss why today is a good time to start thinking about your future.

Lesson 24 What do I need to plan for?

25 What are my career and future opportunities?

Chapter 9 Planning for choices and changes

In this lesson you will:
★ consider factors that may motivate your career choices
★ think more widely about your future career
★ find out where to look for information about careers
★ plan for the future with confidence.

Starter activity

1. Look at the factors in the illustrations below that might influence your choice of career. Put them in order of importance – with 1 being the most important and 6 the least important.
2. Which factors scored most highly in your class?
3. Taken in isolation, should any of these factors alone determine your career choice?

a) Money

b) Prospects (whether you are likely to be able to progress steadily with this career, gaining more responsibility and money)

c) Satisfaction

d) Location (where the career is situated)

e) Flexibility

f) Suitability (whether you have the necessary talents and skills)

52

It is very important to think about your skills, interests and qualities when choosing a future career as well as the financial rewards it might bring. This is because enjoying what you do will make your life happier.

Get Active 1

1. Catherine has no idea what she wants to do when she 'grows up', but she is organised, likes researching projects and is good at maths. List five different types of careers that might suit her talents.
2. As a class, discuss how Catherine's career choices broaden if we take into account that she loves animals and is a caring member of the class.

With so many careers open to you, it might be easy for you to decide not to think about it – after all, you have so much time.

In fact, it is not only exciting thinking about the future but it is never too early to give this subject a little of your attention. Believe it or not, it will help a lot later on.

Get Active 2

1. Draw a spider diagram with you in the centre. At the end of each line, write or illustrate something that you are good at. Take time to look carefully at this information. What conclusions can you draw?
2. Make a list of five careers that you think you could or would like to do based on things you are good at.

Get Active 3

In pairs, compare your careers lists from Get Active 2. Each choose one career that interests you most and list five ways you could find out about this job.

Get Active 4

Is it important to start thinking now about what you might want to do later in life? Give reasons for your answer.

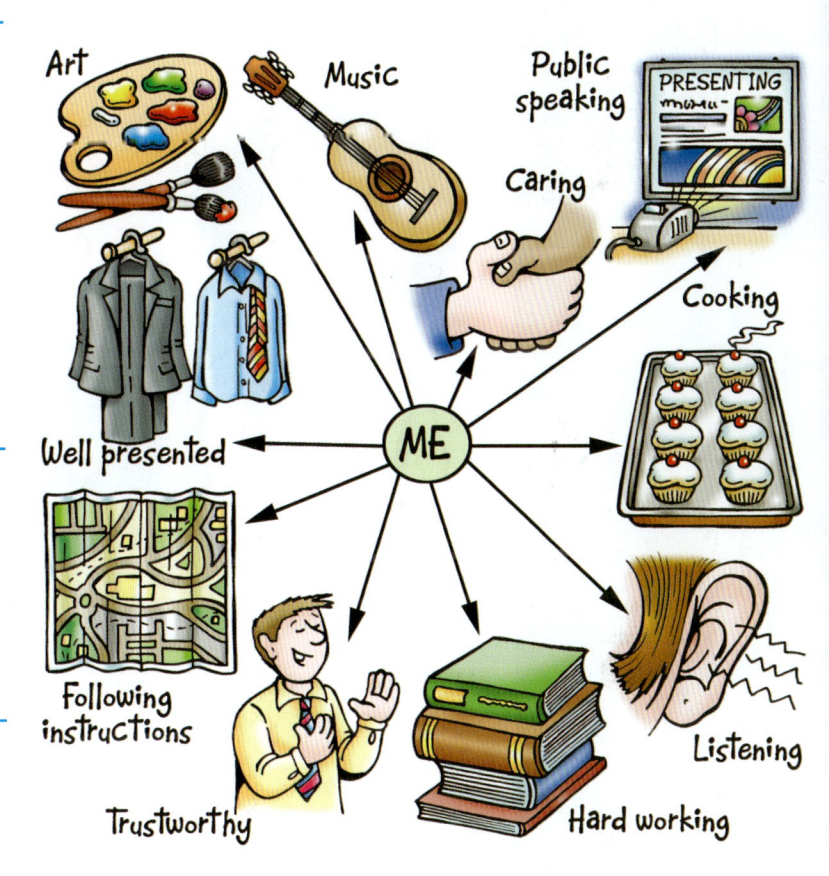

Lesson 25 What are my career and future opportunities?

10 Support and information

26 When and where can we get help?

In this lesson you will:
★ consider the warning signals that tell us when we need help
★ identify some sources of help and support
★ learn about different ways of responding to problem situations.

Starter activity

'The best way to escape from a problem is to solve it.'

- What does this quotation mean?
- Can you think of examples of people you know who have overcome their problems by facing up to them?
- Is it always easy to find a solution?

Facing up to problems isn't easy. Some problems worry or frighten us so much that our bodies react to them physically. Think of the different ways people describe it when this happens:

'I had a sinking feeling.'

'I could feel butterflies in my stomach.'

'I broke out in a cold sweat.'

All these are warning signals made by your body to tell you that you:

- feel at risk
- are worried that you are have a huge problem
- may be facing a new challenge.

Get Active 1

Work with another person to list some other warning signals that people might experience.

We may experience warning signals when we feel unsafe or when we are about to do something unfamiliar or new, for example, when we have to stand up and present a report in class, or audition for a play or sports team. They even happen when we know that at the other end of the experience we may get something good, such as a good grade, a good acting role or a place on the team.

Always pay attention to your warning signals and ask yourself:

- Do I really want to do this thing/take this step?
- What could be the result of doing it?
- Who could I ask for help and support when I do it?

Get Active 2

Where would you advise someone who was experiencing their warning signals to look for information, help or support? Work in pairs to identify where you could go for help:

- in school
- in the local area
- using helplines or other media.

Remember to identify individuals who could help as well as examples of organisations that might be useful.

Get Active 3

Look at The Helping Hand on the right – it suggests five things to do that can help us face up to our problems.

Work in a small group to discuss the five suggestions. Decide which of them might help someone in the following situations and explain how they would do so:

- Getting behind with homework or project work
- Losing or damaging something borrowed from a friend
- Feeling bullied by other pupils.

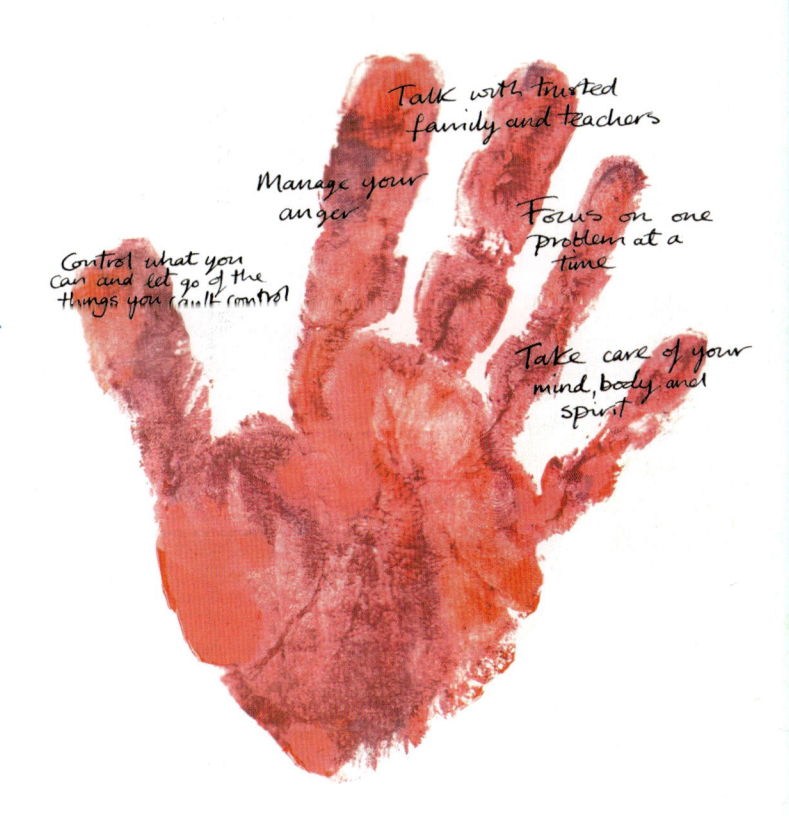

The Helping Hand

(Handprint annotations: Talk with trusted family and teachers; Manage your anger; Control what you can and let go of the things you can't control; Focus on one problem at a time; Take care of your mind, body and spirit)

Get Active 4

Think about suggestion three (the middle finger) on The Helping Hand.

- Who would be your trusted person(s) to turn to for advice?
- Why do you trust them?

Lesson 26 When and where can we get help?

55

27 Where can I find help on …?

Chapter 10 Support and information

> **In this lesson you will:**
> ★ consider the different types of help and support people your age may need
> ★ research some typical sources of help offered to teenagers
> ★ design information for use by pupils in the school.

If you look back over the lessons in this book, you'll find that all the lessons start with a question. These questions are about subjects such as drugs, emotions, HIV, relationships and money.

What other types of Personal, Social and Health questions do you think pupils would like answers to? For example, would they want information about exam worries or friendship problems?

Starter activity
Come up with two or three suggestions of topics that pupils your age might want advice and help on.

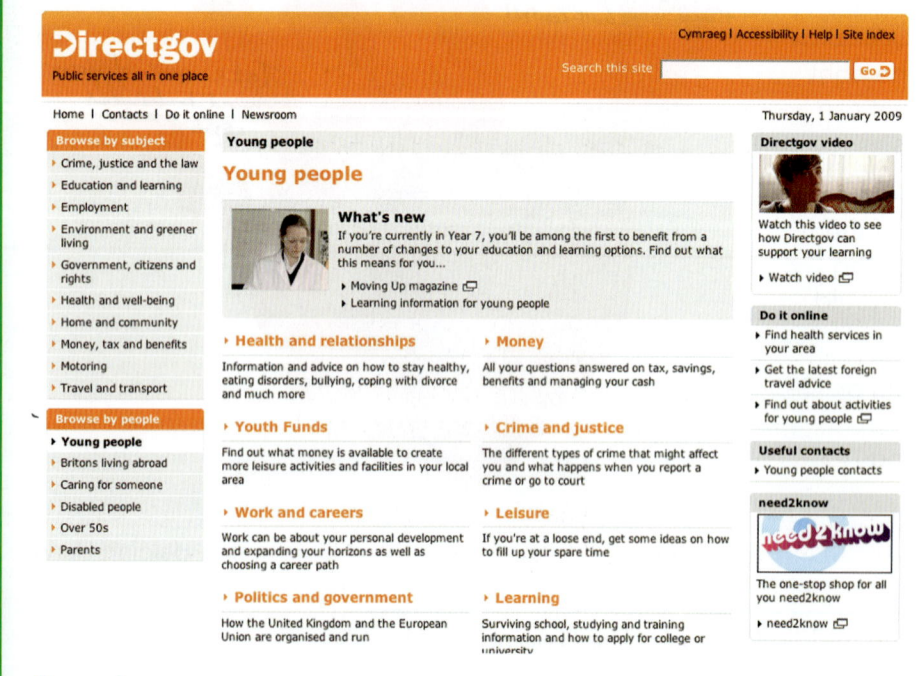

Many websites provide information and support to young people. See Sources 1 and 2 for two examples.

Some websites are easier to use than others and the quality of information varies from site to site. The next activity asks you to investigate some specific and popular sites.

Source 1
Directgov is the digital channel for government communications to citizens. It offers advice and information and gives links to other websites (www.direct.gov.uk)

56

Get Active 1

Working in groups, your task is to look at a source of information for young people. You may be asked to look at one of the websites in Sources 1 or 2 or another one that your teacher will give you.

Your task is to investigate it, sample how it works and produce a review that could help others decide if this is a useful source of advice and help. You will share your review with the rest of the class.

1. Your group should consider the following:
   - Was it easy to read?
   - Was it easy to navigate your way around the website and find more information?
   - Was it interesting to look at?
   - Would you recommend it as a source of help?

   Give examples to explain your responses.

2. Once your group has answered these questions, sum up your review of the website by giving it a score out of ten.
   As a general guide:
   - 3/10 Not very useful, hard to find information, etc.
   - 5/10 Average usefulness – worth a look
   - 7/10 Has got some useful things in it but could be improved (say how)
   - 10/10 Great advice, well presented

Source 2
This is a national charity website that covers all sorts of issues that may affect young people (www.childline.org.uk/)

Get Active 2

Design a poster or web page that highlights some of the sources of information that got high marks in your class. On your poster it should be clear:

- what these sources of information are
- why they are useful
- where people can find them.

Your school may already have a 'help and information' notice board or area of a website for pupils. You could ask for your poster or web page to be displayed there. Remember that you will need to check with the pupils or staff who organise this notice board or area of the website to see if there are special requirements for setting up the information.

If your school doesn't have anything like this, then your year group could take on the task of asking your School Council (or other pupil organisation) to set one up.

Get Active 3

Think back over the lesson. Can you identify a new piece of information or a helping person/agency you hadn't heard of until today?

Lesson 27 Where can I find help on ....?

57

28 Young people's agencies – what do they do?

> In this lesson you will:
> ★ research information about some of the leading agencies that support young people
> ★ present that information to others in the form of a case study.

Starter activity

Before you read any further, answer the following questions. Samaritans is a well-known national agency that provides help and support.

1 What sort of service does Samaritans offer?
2 Who can use the service?

SAMARITANS

We don't know when you might need us.
That's why we're open 24 hours a day.

The aim of the agency

Samaritans provides confidential non-judgemental emotional support, 24 hours a day for people who are experiencing feelings of distress or despair, including those which could lead to suicide.

Samaritans say: 'Whatever you're going through, whether it's big or small, don't bottle it up. We are here for you if you're worried about something, feel upset or confused, or just want to talk to someone.'

The service it offers

People can contact them for support by telephone, email, letter and face to face in most of their branches. Samaritans is available to anyone in the UK and Ireland.

Samaritans is run by

It is a national charity with local branches and local volunteers in most major towns and cities.

Information on their website includes

Details about problems such as depression and how people can be helped; how to volunteer and support Samaritans; contact details for e-mail and local services.

An example of someone who was helped by Samaritans

'One night, around 2am, I phoned Samaritans. A young woman spoke to me but I just didn't know what to say. I couldn't talk about what was happening. So she asked me what I'd done that day and gradually I was able to tell her my story. As I was talking I began to feel a sense of relief as it all came out. When I came off the phone after an hour I was overwhelmed by a feeling of peace and was able to go straight to sleep. It helped so much that I called back the following night. I spoke to a few different volunteers over the next two weeks. It was the same story every night; I just needed to tell someone about it all. They were brilliant, absolutely brilliant. After I phoned Samaritans, I felt more able to get on with my life. After six months … I felt like I could cope.'

People can get in touch with Samaritans to find out more by

Phoning 08457 90 90 90 in the UK or 1850 60 90 90 in the Republic of Ireland* (your local branch number will be in your local directory)

Sending an email to jo@samaritans.org

Visiting www.samaritans.org

Source 1 A case study of a helping agency

*Please see Samaritans website for latest call charge details.

When Samaritans was first set up, there were few agencies that specifically helped young people – today all that has changed. Samaritans is just one of many famous national agencies that can help people when they need someone to turn to. The next activity will look at agencies that particularly offer support to young people.

Get Active 1

1 Look at the chart below showing six agencies that help young people. Your teacher will allocate you one of these agencies and ask you to work with other pupils in a small group. Your task will be to do research, assemble information and present a case study about this agency.

Each one of these agencies could be invaluable to you or other pupils in the future – so this case study could provide crucial awareness of what sort of support is available to someone facing a crisis or difficult time. You could present your case study as:

- a magazine or newspaper article
- a talk with PowerPoint® illustrations
- a radio or television interview with some members of the group as interviewers and others as members of the organisation.

Whatever your format, as in the Samaritans example in Source 1, ensure your case study includes:

- the main aim of the agency
- the services it offers to young people
- information on who runs it (for example, is it a charity or a government department?)
- details of the sort of information you can get online
- an example of someone who received help
- details of how people can get in touch with the agency or find out more.

In your group, remember to plan your work by deciding roles and responsibilities for undertaking various parts of the case study (such as research, creating the presentation slides, speaking, choosing background music if you are using an interview or PowerPoint®).

2 After each group's presentation you may want to offer your feedback. Try to identify:

- at least one thing your group liked about the presentation content
- at least one thing your group liked about the presentation style
- one thing that your group thinks could have improved the presentation content
- one thing that your group thinks could have improved the presentation style.

Get Active 2

If you could invite someone from one of these agencies to come in to school and talk to pupils, which agency would you invite? Why?

Anti-Bullying Alliance www.anti-bullyingalliance.org.uk
Childline www.childline.org.uk
It's not your fault www.itsnotyourfault.org
Think U Know www.thinkuknow.co.uk/11_16/
Young Minds www.youngminds.org.uk/young-people/
Young NCB (National Children's Bureau) www.youngncb.org.uk

11 Review 29

What have I learned?

In this lesson you will:
- ★ review what you have learned in PSHE
- ★ consider your own skills, qualities and achievements
- ★ prepare to move forward into next year.

You have looked at many different issues in this year's PSHE course.

Here are a few of them:

Developing confidence to face challenges

Coping when things go wrong

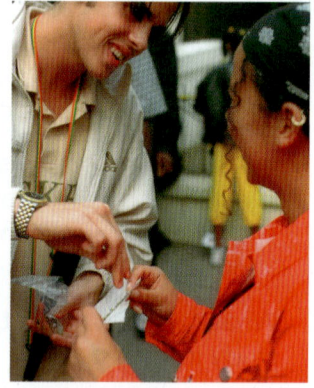

Legal and illegal drugs

Safety and first aid

Relationships, sexual health and parenthood

Starter activity
Think back over the year and jot down one or two things you have enjoyed learning about.

The way we learn in PSHE has changed. The curriculum is now planned to support your health and wellbeing – it consists of 'organisers':

- mental, emotional, social and physical wellbeing
- planning for choices and changes
- relationships, sexual health and parenthood
- substance misuse

In each organiser there are ideas to learn about as well as skills and ways of thinking that support you as you grow up.

Get Active 1

Look back and find an example of something you have learned about each of the following:

a) appreciating differences between yourself and others
b) health – looking after yourself
c) managing your money
d) thinking about your future career
e) your personal qualities.

In Get Active 1 you revisited some of the ideas you have learned about, but you have also developed your skills and ways of thinking over the past year. You have looked at:

a) deciding what to do when faced with a number of choices
b) managing a risky situation
c) developing relationships with other people
d) planning a budget
e) challenging prejudice
f) coping with family disagreements.

Get Active 2

Working in groups, take one of the skills above and come up with some good advice to help another young person develop these skills.

You are ending this school year having gained new knowledge and skills. This final activity asks you to think about how you would sum yourself up at the end of S2.

Get Active 3

Imagine that you have just been given a brand new backpack to carry all your important belongings from this school year into next year. Obviously you will need to take a lot of the information you have learned – but what other important things will you take which reflects who you are?

What would you pack in each of the following pockets? There is room for up to three items in each pocket.

- My Interests
- My Key Skills
- My Personal Qualities
- My Achievements

Get Active 4

Complete this sentence:

'This year I made good progress in PSHE when … '

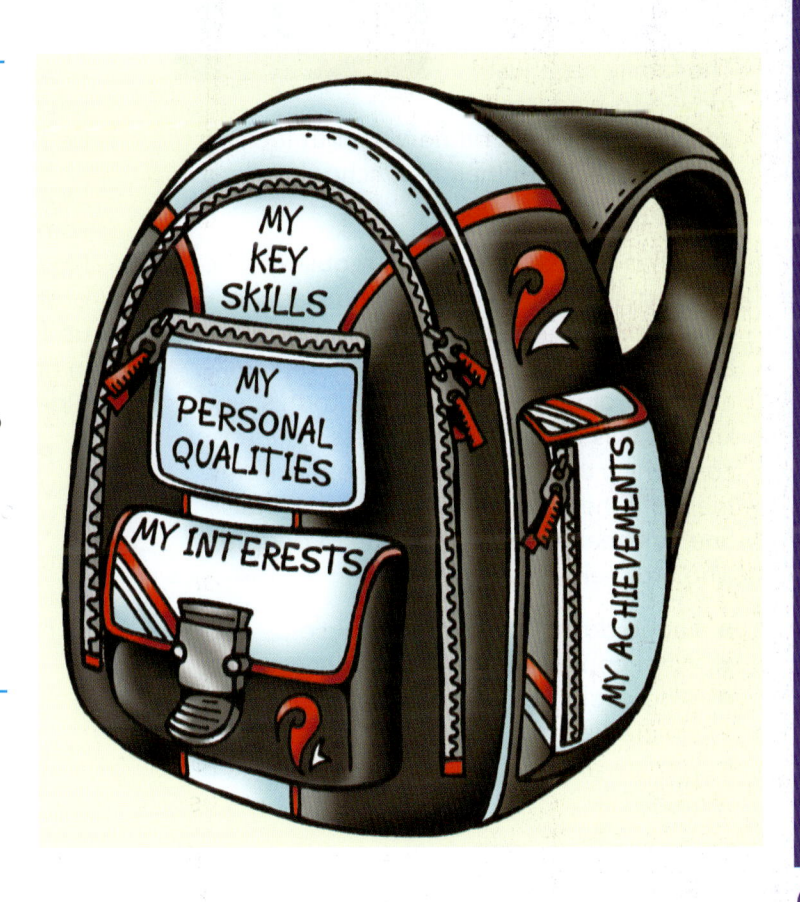

Lesson 29 What have I learned?

How can I keep safe on the inside?

Case studies for Lesson 14

Zachary is thirteen years old and lives with his dad. He has lots of friends and his favourite sport is street hockey. He spends several evenings a week playing with his mates after school. He enjoys school and does well in nearly all his subjects.

Zachary is around at his friend Mark's house with a couple of other mates. Mark wants to show his friends his dad's brilliant new computer. Mark has already been surfing on it and shows the others some adult sites he's found. Zachary is a bit surprised – there's always been something on the computers he's used to stop access to sites like these. He doesn't really like doing this and he feels uncomfortable.

- Zachary doesn't feel safe because …
- What could he do to feel safer?
- Who could he talk to about feeling unsafe?
- Is there anything you would tell Zachary not to do?

Tyler and Laurie are fourteen-year-old twins who live with their mum and dad. The twins have always been popular and have good friends. The family have just moved to a new town and the twins are a bit nervous but looking forward to joining their new school and meeting new people.

Tyler has to take medication regularly. The problem is that if he doesn't, he starts to talk to himself – sometimes in his head and sometimes out loud. Laurie, the family and their old friends were used to this, and knew it was part of Tyler's illness. Laurie is concerned that it will be hard to make new friends if they find out about her brother. She has heard others make fun of people who are mentally ill.

- Laurie doesn't feel safe because …
- What could she do to feel safer?
- Who could she talk to about feeling unsafe?
- Is there anything you would tell Laurie not to do?

Phoenix is twelve and is the youngest of three children, the baby of the family. They all live with their mother. Phoenix did well in First Year at school but now that his older brother and sister have left he wonders what it will be like in Second Year.

Last week, Phoenix got pushed around by some older pupils and one took his money. Now that he's at school without his older brother and sister he thinks he should stand up for himself. He wonders if having a knife in his pocket will help him stand up to the older pupils.

- Phoenix doesn't feel safe because …
- What could he do to feel safer?
- Who could he talk to about feeling unsafe?
- Is there anything you would tell Phoenix not to do?